QUALITY BOOK FORMULA

PROFESSIONALLY PUBLISH YOUR BOOK FOR EXCELLENCE

BRIGITTE CUTSHALL

THIS BOOK IS DEDICATED TO CARL

He's not only my husband, but that guy who built a huge bookshelf from scratch for me in our home. He knows that I love books just as much as I love him.

Table of Contents

Note from the Author

Books have always fascinated me. I view physical books as an expression of creativity. Words on paper. It's art.

But, more importantly, a book can help clarify your brand—who you are and what you do— and put it squarely in front of the readers who need your expertise.

Growing up, friends referred to me as that 'book girl' because I was always holding a book and reading. Digital devices didn't exist then.

Our parents always had books available for us to read. Even though we didn't have a lot of money, we always had access to books. Books kept my curiosity and creativity awake. Books were also an escape. They still are.

The spare room upstairs is where our parents kept a bookshelf filled with mostly hardcover books. That room was next to my bedroom, and I referred to it as 'the library' and spent a lot of time there reading on a blue bean bag chair. It was the '70s.

My main source of information as a kid was a physical set of encyclopedias (this was long before the internet). I was fascinated by the Encyclopedia Britannica (EB) our parents bought us. And, if I remember correctly, ours was a twenty-six-volume set. That is a memorable book brand because I still remember it.

Encyclopedias were very popular—they'd been around since the Middle Ages—and you were considered rich if you could afford a set at home. I'm pretty sure our parents paid installments on ours. Those types of books were a reliable educational tool.

Encyclopedia Britannica was not only a publisher but also a book printer. It used to be common for publishers to own printing equipment. EB was established in England (hence Britannica) in 1768 to compete with a French version. The British publisher wanted to prove they were better.

I recall those books being very large and heavy, a trim size of 8.5" x 11", with a leather cover and foil stamping on the spine and front cover.

If I got into a minor argument with someone (my brother, for example), I would run into our library and pull one of the encyclopedia volumes off the shelf. I'd look up the topic that I wanted to back up my argument—the books were titled by the alphabet letters—with the goal to prove him wrong.

It's basically what we do with a Google search on the internet now.

I can't say enough how much books have had a positive impact on my life—more so than newspapers or magazines. A book fascinated me with the way it felt in my hands for some reason. It was like magic because it contained stories, different perspectives, and knowledge.

I am still very fascinated with books. Maybe that is why I always inspect the quality of a book after those experiences holding leather Encyclopedia Britannica books in my hand as a child. The weight, the smell of leather, the texture of foil stamping on the cover. It is quality art.

MANY DECADES LATER, I'M STILL KNOWN AS "THE BOOK GIRL."

I want to publish a book. Where do I start?

Many people ask this question since I've been in the book business for most of my adult life. There are many steps and nuances in the process of creating a book. It can be overwhelming to those who aren't familiar.

I decided to write this book after feedback from others that I get excited when talking about books. "Share your knowledge, Brigitte!"

Producing a book is an act of collaboration. You need input from others to complete it. For example, the author, the editor, the designer, and the printer all must be on the same page. It's a delicate balance.

I've learned over the years that the steps to produce a book can be achieved through a simple formula. A formula is a powerful way to capture a working solution.

WHAT'S THE PURPOSE OF A BOOK THESE DAYS?

That's a complex question.

Books do many things. It's not just about applying ink to paper then weighing that paper down through binding so that the paper doesn't blow away.

Books serve one purpose for the writer and another for the reader.

As the writer of this book, *Quality Book Formula*, my purpose is to share the experience and knowledge of thirty plus years in the print media industry, focused on book production. My goal is to help others understand the elements of what makes a quality book by making the best, and correct production choices, especially for printed books.

Although it's an essential element, this book is not going to dive into the writing process.

Creating a great and memorable book is a combination of art, craft, and science. It's a quality book formula with individual elements. I'll dive deeper into each element.

What is the purpose for you, the reader of this book? I think it is to be aware of and understand the elements involved in creating a quality book. In addition, you may have a different reason for why you are interested in or even want to create a book.

In general, your readers want (maybe even crave) a curated, packaged, and delivered content experience. There is a large ocean of content competing for attention, so the essence of your book is important, and that will help distinguish your brand.

My intent is to keep you engaged while reading *Quality Book Formula*. At the end of this book there is a Reflective Notes section and I recommend you write down any thoughts or ideas. This will help you reflect and provide focus for your next book project!

CHAPTER ONE

A Book Is More Than Words. It's Part Of Your Brand.

Branding sounds corporate but it's not.

"Your brand" is how you package and present your message, an essential component of marketing. Books are an integral part of print media and print media is a tactic used as part of a marketing strategy. Branding is the cornerstone.

Visual and communication guidelines are important to create consistency with your message. Guidelines at a minimum include logo design, colors, and specific fonts.

A brand is *not* just your logo or a document with design guidelines.

To me, the definition of brand is the distinctive identity of a product or service. There are thousands of products and services available in many industries and your brand helps attract attention, allowing it to stand out from the clutter.

A brand can create and stand for loyalty, trust, faith, premium or mass-market appeal. For example, a brand differentiates a product from other similar products. This distinction makes it possible to charge a higher premium in return for that clearer identity. Also, a brand is more likely to survive longer than a generic offering that is undifferentiated and blends in.

Think of a brand as a living being. It can be you. You have an identity and personality, a name and culture, vision, emotion, and intelligence. All these traits are conveyed by the owner of a brand and should be consistent to stay relevant for the intended audience.

A physical book can help showcase your uniqueness, personality, and expertise. A book can also build trust with readers and future clients. It can be an effective part of your marketing strategy.

The relationship between print and digital products is the balancing act of our current situation. The rise of digital print technology makes it easier to write and produce your own book.

Our world is heavily invested in digital media and information technology, but print media is still relevant. Perhaps one reason is the convenience of reading something any time you want that physical copies provide.

The quality of a book, especially a physical version, is important and can impact your brand. It's tied to your marketing plan and strategy. I can't emphasize this enough. You don't want to be remembered negatively because your book looks like crap.

Creating a book is quite an endeavor, and many people are respected for being an author, even if it's just one book. Every author learns that there is a process to follow—a basic strategy to make it from the idea of a book to publishing the book. It requires a time commitment, some money, and some help.

You need to respect the process. Successful authors learn from their mistakes, and authors, in general, learn that you can't do it alone because it takes a team to make it happen. Understanding how this all works can ease the creation and planning process of your book. There are no shortcuts.

Publishing a book is like an adventure. Keeping that in mind allows the process to be more fun and less daunting. By the way, when 'daunting' is what they're focused on, many potential authors give up. But that doesn't have to happen.

You invest a lot of time (and money) in every step, and each step is connected. It's important to have not just quality writing but quality production and design.

From my perspective, and with experience helping produce over 300 million books since the early '90s, creating a book can be broken down into three main sections:

QUALITY BOOK FORMULA:

DEVELOPMENT

+

PRODUCTION

+

MARKETING

CHAPTER TWO

STEPS TO CREATING AN EXCELLENT BOOK YOU CAN BE PROUD OF

DEVELOPMENT

Communication and collaboration from the beginning with your team

- Understand the goal of your book, the foundation
- Who's going to benefit?
  - o Who is your audience?
  - o What is the end-user value?
- Do the writing
- The editing process
  - o Line editing
  - o Copy editing
  - o Proofreading

- Develop a Budget Plan early on for production
  - o Design
  - o Production method (offset or digital)
  - o Pre-production
    - Copyright
    - ISBN
    - Library of Congress
    - Counterfeit protection
  - o What book formats?
    - Physical, eBook, Audio

PRODUCTION

- Design - cover and interior
  - o Choose the right designer
  - o Improper design is a headache for you and the printer and wasting money.
  - o Great print design is a combination of visual appeal and technical precision.
- Physical books
  - o Print method
  - o Trim Size - standard or slightly different (to make it stand out)
  - o Paper - choice is affected and connected by the design
  - o Binding
  - o Packaging

- Other book formats to consider
  - o eBook
  - o Audio

MARKETING

- It's basically about letting others know why they should buy your book.
- Engage with your audience. It is important to foster connections and relationships.
- Marketing is a never-ending process that can be hard for some; includes planning and consistent action.
- Choose your publishing method early in the process.
- Choose your distribution channels.

CHAPTER THREE

DEVELOPMENT

WHY THE CONTENT OF YOUR BOOK
MATTERS SO MUCH

Book development simply starts with an idea. That idea can turn into many things: for example, fiction books or nonfiction books, children's books, photography books, or cookbooks. There are so many options.

I've always been a big fan of reading fiction over the years. They are a way to escape and take a break from your responsibilities for a few hours. So many genres are available. My favorite is historical fiction like *The Book Thief.*

Nonfiction books, in particular, are very popular now because they usually try to help solve a common pain point. It's amazing the topics that are available. I have been reading more nonfiction for the last five or so years, because I yearn to learn as I age.

Fiction books have a different writing process compared to nonfiction. I'm not going to dive into this difference because that is not my expertise.

But I do know that you need to understand your goals—or have a main goal—for developing and writing a book. Having this awareness is basically having the end in mind, which will help you develop the outline or main points in the type of book you choose to write.

You also need to consider the value you're providing to the end-user. Having a value statement for your book early on will help with the writing process and marketing plan.

Doing some research on what you plan to write about is an important step. It will help with the outline and main points you want to touch on. You need to have a clear picture of the subject and content. Research will help organize your thoughts, craft narratives, or support an argument (point) you are trying to convey.

The writing process is different for everyone. It depends on what else is happening in your life and relates to the end goal(s) for your book.

a. What are your goals or the main goal?

o The answers to this are also part of your marketing plan.

    b. Writer's block is real, and managing your book as a project will help.

        o I recommend reading Project Management for Writers (by Terry Stafford) to help overcome it.

    c. Get a mentor or coach. At a minimum, team up with an accountability partner. It will help with motivation in the writing process.

Understanding your goals and the end-user value helps build the foundation for the book. I'm not going to dive into the craft of writing in this book. You will find a way to make the writing part happen and make it to the editing stage.

EDITING – WHY EDITING IS ESSENTIAL TO CREATE AN EXCELLENT BOOK

The best writers you read use the best editors. They spend the money for "fresh eyes" because they know a great editor can take their work and make it better.

Anne Lamott in her book, *Bird by Bird*, talks about your "sh***y first draft". EVERYONE has one. (Including me - I've used three editors so far as I'm writing this to make this book better.)

But how do you find the "right" editor for you? (You may have to interview a few to find the right one that fits best for your situation.)

The editing stage is one of the most important elements in publishing a book. Any book out there will most likely have a few errors, even the traditionally published books. If you have a lot of errors and typos—more than a dozen—most readers will notice, and that is not a high-quality product. It can affect your credibility.

The more sets of eyes you have to review the content before designing and printing, the better. We're all human, and mistakes happen. There are several types of editors, and knowing the options are important in the manuscript development stage.

1. Developmental Editing: The goal here is to shape the manuscript, so the editor can re-write and ask for more clarification. They polish the manuscript. For this type of editing, it's best to use someone who understands the topic you're writing about.

   You can take this route if you're uncomfortable with writing. Developmental editing is expensive because it is intensive, and most *New York Times* bestsellers have this type of editing provided.

2. Line Editing: A line editor edits a manuscript line by line, focusing on tone and flow. Line editors consider the author's intended message and suggest changes in word choice and tone

to increase the impact of that message. Line editing is sometimes called stylistic editing.

3. Copyediting: The editor here basically reads the document to make sure the structure is correct, including grammar and punctuation. They will also give you feedback if the content or message isn't clear. They do not re-write but can ask the author questions for clarification. Is it clear and concise? Sometimes it involves fact checking.

4. Proofreading: Proofreading is always the last step in a good editing process. It is essential and the simplest but still requires a sharp eye and attention to detail. Proofreading deals with grammar, spelling, typographical errors, and readability of the book during design layout. It is the final review before going to print.

Editing services and freelancers usually charge by word count or by the hour. Pricing increases with the depth of the project and with the types of editing involved.

Proofreading is the least expensive step but still very critical. It's common for many manuscripts to go through several revisions before the editing process is complete.

PRE-PRODUCTION: PUTTING A PLAN TOGETHER TO PROTECT YOUR BOOK CONTENT

This is the phase where you have the writing complete, editing is basically done, and you're getting the manuscript prepared for design and actual production.

You need to be aware of the following four elements before book production:

1. Copyright protection

2. ISBN registration

3. Library of Congress (option)

4. Counterfeit prevention

COPYRIGHT PROTECTION - AND MANAGING RIGHTS

The foundation of copyrighting content begins with you, the author, as you start the creative process of writing. You own the intellectual property.

Your work is protected under intellectual property law from the moment your words are written on paper or saved to a digital file. It doesn't require a formal registration anymore. A copyright is literally 'the right' to copy a work. With copyright, content (a work) can be copied (used) only if the owner gives permission. It provides the owner of a body of work the ability to decide how and when others may use it.

Copyright law makes it easier for authors to make money selling their books. It prevents a bookstore, for example, from buying one copy of a book, making copies of that book, and then selling those copies to their customers.

At a minimum, you must have a copyright notice at the beginning of your book. It's exactly why it's referred to as the copyright page. *The very existence of a copyright notice will discourage infringement.*

When a publication includes a valid copyright notice, an infringer can't claim that they didn't know it was copyrighted.

Also, including a copyright notice can make it easier for someone to track down the copyright owner and obtain permission to use the work legitimately.

WHAT IS A VALID COPYRIGHT NOTICE?

A copyright notice should contain:

- the word "copyright" or
- "c" in a circle (©)
- the date of publication, and
- the name of either the author or the owner of all the rights in the published work.

For example, you own your copyright just by claiming it simply like this:

© 2021 by Brigitte Cutshall

OR

Copyright 2021 by Brigitte Cutshall

In the United States, a copyright owner can significantly enhance the protection by registering the copyright with the U.S. Copyright Office.

Copyright law is a little complicated.

- You can't copyright a book title, and theoretically, you can reuse *The Book Thief* title, for example, but it's not advised.
- You can't use a book title that has been trademarked. Some titles are registered and trademarked as a book series like *Harry Potter.*
- You can access content when the copyright has expired, seventy years after the author dies; then it becomes a work in the public domain.

I'm not an attorney, but I recommend that you register your copyright. As writers, we have an obligation to respect the law. It will also put your book in line with professional publishing. Register here: https://www.copyright.gov/

Here's a link to download a PDF with more detail of the copyright basics in the U.S.:

https://www.copyright.gov/circs/circ01.pdf

ISBN REGISTRATION

An ISBN (International Standard Book Number) is assigned to every trade book published to make it unique in the marketplace. But it doesn't mean an ISBN is officially the copyright of your book. And it's not just a bar code either.

It's recommended that you own your ISBNs if you are self-publishing because each sale of the different products (editions) is tracked and associated with the publisher. And that's you.

Know that each edition of a book needs its own ISBN: hardcover version, softcover version, eBook, and audio. An ISBN is needed for audiobooks if you plan to sell it through physical stores and libraries. Note that if you update content in the future as a new edition, a new ISBN is needed. An ISBN can never be reused. Many people aren't aware of this.

Side note: My understanding is that you don't have to use an ISBN on Amazon for eBooks or Audiobooks because they assign ASIN's to them. If you distribute your content on other platforms, you will still need an ISBN though.

Each country has a different organization for assigning ISBNs. You obtain an ISBN for the country where your writing or publishing business is located. Bowker manages the registrations in the United States. Go here to check it out: https://isbn.org/

I learned from my friend, Fredrick Haugen, that the Canadian Federal Government provides an ISBN for free…probably to encourage people to write books.

LIBRARY OF CONGRESS CONTROL NUMBER

This is another step to take for your book to be professional. Professionally published books include a LOC (Library of Congress) number on the copyright page. The goal here is to make your book easier to be discovered by librarians and bookstores.

It's a simple process. You apply online to the LOC to include a digital copy of your book. You are then assigned a CIP number (CIP stands for Cataloging In Publication). You then add that number as a separate line to your copyright page. It can take about a week to receive your control number.

When a physical copy is available, you mail that in for verification.

The Library of Congress Registration step is not required but can open some doors to new readers. Start here - https://loc.gov/publish/

COUNTERFEIT PREVENTION

Counterfeiting a product is not new and has been around forever. If your idea or product is popular and successful, someone will try to copy it to earn some money. Be prepared.

As a health advocate, I've always acknowledged prevention methods and pointed out the benefits. That type of approach can be applied to many things, including book production.

Printing is a valuable and versatile platform that provides communication methods, identification, and interaction. Securing print is increasingly important as we continue to see increased counterfeiting and a need for brand protection.

With the rise of digital printing, it has become easier for counterfeit books to occur because the cost is lower to reproduce—digital equipment is very inexpensive and small enough in size to have one in your garage. Something that is counterfeited is not excellent quality.

The most common type of content that is affected by counterfeiting is related to educational and training material.

So, what are my recommended counterfeit prevention methods?

Here's a list I created based on issues that have occurred with clients.

1. Copyright protection. The prospect of counterfeit is another reason to officially copyright your work.

2. Consider using lay-flat binding (Otabind) for your book. The gap created in the binding process *cannot* be replicated via the digital print method. (I will explain more about this later.)

3. 50# Smooth white offset text paper is the most common paper for digital printing because it is inexpensive. Use a natural or cream color paper or a vellum finish or bump it up to 60# smooth white paper at least. (In the Production section, I dive more into paper options.)

4. You can add a *small* tamper-evident label to the outside covers. If a counterfeiter tries to remove the label, it will shred and affect the cover material. They won't be able to scan the cover in a high-quality manner.

5. Have the designer include graphics in the interior that will be difficult to scan.

6. Include a hidden image in the interior that is not visible in the design, like a 2D barcode.

7. Include a card that has a security scratch-off panel. This is usually for when you are giving the book buyer access to online content.

   a. The card format is standard business card size, and the card can be applied with a glue dot inside the front cover.

    b. Or the "card" security info can be printed directly on the inside cover (this can be done now via digital printing)

At a minimum, sign up for Amazon brand registry. A lot of counterfeit books have been sold on the Amazon platform. It will help to make a counterfeit claim easier. https://brandservices.amazon.com/

Chapter Four

Production

CONNECTING THE RESOURCES
TO CREATE YOUR BOOK

You want your book to stand out because of its excellent quality.

The word 'excellent' makes me think of *Bill & Ted's Excellent Adventure*—a science-fiction comedy movie that throws in some history lessons. It's one of my favorite movies because the genre is historical fiction.

Bill & Ted's Excellent Adventure now has several accompanying hardcover children books. These books consist of original illustrations, four-color pictures, advice on how to live a non-heinous life, how to make friends, etc. That is an excellent way to repurpose content into a book and an example of a brand's extension.

Repurposing content is something to consider as part of your brand. It depends on the audience you relate to and what they want.

Production includes many detailed steps—final editing of content, design and layout, and the manufacturing process (size, material, and finishing)—to turn that book idea into an actual product.

It's the details that make a difference and can make your book stand out.

It's recommended that books have multiple formats now—physical book, eBook, and audiobook. You can increase the outreach to readers based on offering different formats. Some people want to hold a physical book, some want a digital version to read on a phone or tablet, and others want to just listen.

A physical book requires the actual manufacturing of printing on paper and binding those pages together. Just writing that statement brings back visual memories of being in huge printing plants for tours with clients, press checks, and equipment presentations.

Those pressrooms had some massive offset presses that were long and loud. It was a bit mesmerizing for me to watch the huge blank rolls of paper go into the machine in the front and come out the other end printed with ink on the paper.

Depending on the type of equipment, the output had the pages folded inline (a printing term called a signature), and the signatures rolled along the conveyor belt to stack up at the end for the binding stage.

There are so many different trim size formats and material (paper) options; it can become overwhelming to those who aren't familiar. The process can become overwhelming for people when they get deep in the weeds and become stuck because they aren't sure how to proceed.

Book manufacturing depends a lot on the budget as the baseline. There are standard sizes, standard materials, and standard finishing or binding options. Finishing and binding are called the post-press stage.

In addition, you need to consider the production timeline in your book plan. The quantity ordered and type of book (softcover, hardcover, digital print, or offset print) affects the number of days needed for production turnaround. Plus, don't forget, you need to consider the timeframe for delivery logistics.

Setting expectations are important. Don't expect to place a large book print order and have it ready to ship in a week. Larger quantities require a longer turnaround and are affected by paper availability and the printer's internal manufacturing schedule.

The word 'large' is a bit vague. Large print runs usually reference web offset printing, which is 5000 copies or more. Many people have asked what the standard turnaround time is. My answer depends on which print method you use (digital vs. offset) and the type of binding you choose (softcover vs. hardcover).

Digital book printing turnaround time is less and can average seven business days for a softcover book after proofs are approved. Turnaround time is mostly related to the manufacturing press-time available, the availability of material (paper), and the print quantity.

A frame of reference for offset printing:

- The average for a softcover book is three to four weeks produced via offset press plus shipping time.
- The average for a hardcover book is five to six weeks produced via offset press plus shipping time. The hardcover binding process has extra post-press production steps.

Note: There have been longer lead times to get paper due to the effects on the supply chain due to the COVID-19 pandemic starting in 2020.

Technology has also affected the manufacturing options in good and bad ways; it depends on your perspective. I'll focus on the good.

I'm about to get a little technical here but will try to go easy on the jargon.

PRINT METHODS

The print industry has historically used the offset printing method.

If you're not familiar with that term, offset printing is a technique that involves the transfer of an image from a metal plate to a rubber blanket before being printed (applied) on the paper or other substrate. Offset is also called lithography.

Lithography was invented around 1796 by Johann Alois Senefelder, a playwright from Munich. He loved writing but the cost to produce printed plays was expensive. At the time, the process (invented by Gutenberg) required using a letterpress and engraving.

Senefelder discovered that using copper plates and greasy ink repelled water. This method costs less than engraving, provides more vibrant colors, and can print larger quantities at the same time.

Offset has been around for over 225 years and the print quality of the method is still exceptional. Now, however, it is considered a more expensive process compared to digital print because there is usually a minimum print run to be cost-efficient.

Offset print also provides a lot more options regarding trim sizes and paper.

So what about the modern day process of digital printing?

Digital print was first introduced around 1993, and the print industry has never been the same. It was created to produce short print runs that were cost-effective. The main difference is that digital presses do not use printing plates; computer software is used to manage a print run, not a pressman.

The only downside is that there is a loss of detail (particularly in photos) when not using a printing plate. That could change in the future. This loss of detail could make a difference in quality if your book design is photo heavy.

The print media industry, especially book production, is embracing the digital print method now because the print quality has improved substantially since the early '90s.

In addition to using paper, digital printing can be used with different substrates like vinyl and fabric. This is why the promotional products industry has skyrocketed.

Digital now includes two types of processes—inkjet printing and laser printing. The difference is that inkjet printers use ink cartridges and laser printers use cartridges with toner powder.

Inkjet printers spray microscopic droplets of ink onto paper. They generally cost less and are smaller in size. They are used to print text and high-quality colored images, especially photos.

Laser printers melt toner powder on paper to create a print. Laser printers are more expensive than inkjet upfront; the toner cartridges cost more but are more economical in the long run because of the faster printing speeds.

If a lot of photos are involved, and you want to go the digital route, inkjet printing is recommended as a higher quality option than laser (at least right now).

Also, keep in mind that photos need to be printed at a minimum of 300dpi (dots per inch) no matter the print process—offset or digital. Designers should know that already, but it's an important reminder.

Inkjet presses are now being manufactured in wide format options to compete even better with the offset press. The standard size for a digital inkjet press has traditionally been 12" x 18" sheets, and wide format is at least 24". This capability keeps getting updated and depends on the manufacturer.

POD (PRINT ON DEMAND)

Because offset printing usually requires a minimum run length of 1,000 copies, there has been a massive shift in publishing to shorter print run lengths.

Print On Demand (POD) with the modern digital printing processes has cut run lengths to as little as 25 copies or even one copy to order depending on the plant. POD is often referred to as a web-to-print application.

Replacing traditional long-run lengths with efficient shorter digital runs is the new supply-and-demand mantra. The benefit for publishers is that they will be able to accommodate an entirely new client market. It's also a win-win for printing companies and book publishers who can keep titles in print longer while eliminating inventory costs.

POD is considered a cost-effective way to print high-quality books and is very flexible regarding fulfillment. Fulfillment is simply the process of packaging and shipping book orders, usually to an individual customer.

There will be some trim size limits based on the current equipment that exists, but that's okay. That is an example where you need to reach out early to a printer to determine the trim size options and paper options they offer.

The POD production method also allows for personalization capabilities. Personalized print is like the Wild West now because you can customize the design for individual copies and create your book anyway you want thanks to POD.

An example of personalization: one of my clients had partners include their branded logo on the back covers that required a minimum order of 100 copies each time. It was a hit. Two brands on one book cover increased the market exposure for their collaborative message.

WHAT PRINTER (PRODUCTION PLANT) SHOULD I USE?

Who you chose for production is based on the design and your budget.

Reach out to a book printer as early as possible. It's important to help with budget development, narrow down your costs, and get your designer's input. Many printing plants have both print methods in-house—offset and digital equipment.

My recommendation is to ask for a printed physical sample (or two) from a printer because you will be able to check out the expected quality. I also like to ask what type of press and post-press equipment they have since that can affect the end-quality. That's just me.

I don't recommend using a commercial printer to produce a perfect-bound book. They can produce brochures or saddle stitch booklets effectively. Understand that their post-press equipment is usually a standalone folder, saddle stitchers, and a type of coil binding.

Commercial printers normally don't have the resources to afford perfect binding equipment in-house. If they accept a perfect-bound book project from you, they will usually outsource the binding to another plant.

That outsourcing aspect adds to the schedule and logistics timeline. Plus, you'll have some shipping costs included to get the printed signatures delivered to the binding plant.

Choose a printer specializing in book production because they have invested in the right equipment to produce quality books. That is their specialty.

Printing equipment is expensive, and so is the binding (post-press) equipment, especially a perfect binder and hardcover equipment.

WHAT ARE MY BOOK BINDING OPTIONS?

I had some visuals created to help explain the book binding options better.

Perfect bound - With perfect binding, the folded pages are trimmed with the softcover forming 'perfect' edges. People love this method for the combination of good looks and low cost.

A perfect binder has multiple pockets that the folded print text signatures are placed into. The signatures from the press are stacked on top of each other on a conveyor belt; glue is applied on the bound edge; the cover is wrapped around the stack; then a final trim/cut occurs at the end.

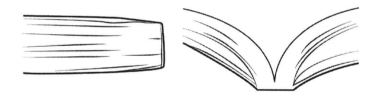

Smyth sewn binding - This type of binding is considered the highest quality bookbinding and most secure. Smyth sewn means that the folded signatures off the press are literally sewn with durable thread, then glued to the cover. The text pages lay flatter when a book is opened and very durable. This binding method can be used for softcover and hardcover books.

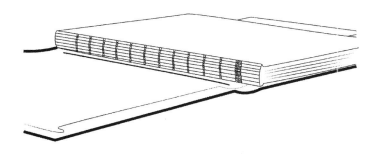

Hardcover/Case-bound - This style can be a tuxedo for books. It's about showcasing quality. Hardcover binding provides the best protection and has an unmatched appearance. Your books will last for many years.

There are two options for hardcover: adhesive casebound and smyth-sewn binding. Smythe-sewn is the top of the line, as mentioned above.

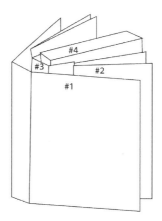

1. The case includes three boards (front, back, and spine) covered with paper or cloth material.
2. The end sheets attach the book block to the case.
3. Gauze strip keeps the spine aligned with the end sheets and book block.
4. The book block is made of the text signatures sewn or glued together.

Otabind (lay-flat) Bound - Otabind is like case-binding using a paper cover. You "hang" the text block on the cover paper with hinges. There is less surface area (a gap) where the glue adheres to hinges attached to the cover instead of glue completely applied to the spine. This binding is where very durable glue is needed.

Saddle stitch - A highly cost-effective way to bind a book is saddle stitching. This method stacks all the pages on top of one another then staples the pages together through the centerfold with the cover on the outside. The max page count depends on the paper used; 64 text pages max on average for this.

Coil bound - Coil or spiral-bound books are bound by punching holes along the edges of the sheets then winding a coil through them. It is simple and inexpensive. It's quick too.

You have the option for wire coil, double wire, and plastic wire coil. There are color options for the wire you can choose from. Double wire coil is very heavy duty and recommended for large books.

Single wire coil

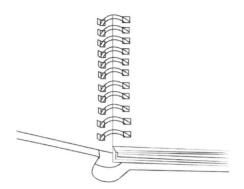

Double wire coil

Plastic-coil

GBC Bound - GBC binding punches holes in the edge of the sheets before binding all the pages together with a simple plastic spine. Sometimes simple is best.

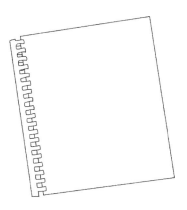

GLUE MATTERS TOO

Some people have experienced bad bookbinding; it's not just about the quality of the print. Most of the time, if a book falls apart, it's because the wrong type of glue was used to keep costs down for the book manufacturer.

Once, a client was referred to me because their perfect-bound books were falling apart. It was a training company that used the physical book as part of the classroom training. Not a good look or perception if the teaching method (the book) falls apart.

Did I mention having a book fall apart is not a quality representation for your brand?

These books were 8.5" x 11" format, and the page count was over 400 text pages. That is a heavy book and a lot of weight in the binding area. They had used a local commercial printer, not a printer that specialized in book production. But the client was not aware that the type of glue used matters with something that large and heavy.

A question to ask a book printer, especially if you're going to have a large perfect-bound book, is what type of adhesive they use? PUR is considered the best. PUR Binding refers to a softcover bookbinding method that uses polyurethane reactive adhesive.

PUR binding is the most durable bookbinding glue available. It is much better than Ethylene Vinyl Acetate (EVA) or any other adhesives used in traditional perfect binding. PUR glue is used 100% of the time with Otabinding (lay-flat).

DESIGN AND LAYOUT OF A BOOK - HOW TO MAKE YOUR BOOK EASY FOR THE READER TO READ

There are a lot of designers out there and some might want the book to look artsy and cool. But is that going to be effective for the reader?

The design of a book is what connects the reader by drawing *positive* attention to it. This element is critical and where you should get assistance from a designer that specializes in books.

You have the cover and interior (text) pages, and each has its own variables to deal with.

COVER DESIGN

You need to do some research because book cover design is an art by itself. I don't recommend that you design your own cover unless you are a graphic artist with specific experience.

There are nuances that non-cover book designers aren't aware of or don't understand. Most books these days are in different formats to include physical and digital. The cover design needs to consider that too.

Cover designs are very genre-specific, which requires a strong familiarity with the book publishing and marketing industry.

Most professionally designed books are simple, and they don't stand out as a poor design. That's the point. The power of design is to be subtle and not draw negative attention.

The cover graphics can include photos or simple graphics. If you use a photo, I recommend using your own because you own the rights to that photo. There are photo sites you can choose pictures from, but there are legal limits. (I use my own photos for the books that I publish.)

Make sure any photo used is high resolution, minimum of 300 dpi.

The cover layout depends on the number of interior pages, trim size of the book, and type of paper used. A standard perfect-bound book cover has three sections: front cover, spine, and back cover.

It goes another level if you plan to produce a hardcover book with a dust jacket. Traditional hardcover books are boards wrapped with cloth or paper material and foil stamped on the spine and front cover. Then there is a dust jacket to wrap around, requiring flaps to tuck in the front and back.

Once the trim size is confirmed and the interior page count is finalized, your designer will need a template for the cover, normally provided by the printer. That will ensure the final quality design of the cover by identifying the print area, bleed requirements, etc.

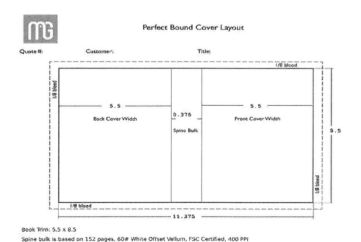

Cover template example (courtesy of McNaughton & Gunn)

The front cover design is usually done prior to the interior because it can provide inspiration for the interior layout. Interior design impacts the margins and bleeds.

The spine design for a perfect bound is based on the final width. This is simple content: book title, author name, and a logo. Sometimes it can be hard to read if the font used is *too small*. Keep that in mind and make sure the font is readable.

Don't know any designers? Ask other authors for references and look at their previous work (portfolio). You can find some great freelance cover designers on Upwork.com. These people make a living at graphic design.

INTERIOR PAGES

Your manuscript is done, and editing is complete. You have a final page count and trim size chosen. That is when you need to consider the production elements for the interior.

You want the book to be easy to read, so again, one of the critical variables to consider is the font. There are a lot of font options now and sticking to a simple font is best.

Interior design is also affected by how the content is produced:

- the trim size
- black & white or 4-color interior
- type of paper chosen
- binding style

A different designer is normally used for the interior pages. But I've seen it done both ways: (1) a different cover designer and a different interior designer; (2) a designer to handle both the cover and interior. It depends on your budget and the experience of the designer.

BOOK TRIM SIZE

There are a lot of trim-size options available. The options depend on the book printer and the type of equipment they have. Using a standard trim size can help keep the cost down. For example, a 6" x 9" trim size will have fewer text pages than a 5" x 8" format... you are using less paper.

The most common trade paperback sizes are 5" x 8", 5.5" x 8.5" and 6" x 9".

Mass paperback books are smaller in format at 4.25" x 6.87".

The most common hardcover book formats range from 6" x 9" to 8.5" x 11".

Also, you should consider the popular traditional publishing book category your book fits into. Here is a shortlist of standard sizes by category:

- 5" x 7" (YA fiction)
- 5" x 8" (inspirational)
- 5.25" x 8" (memoirs; general self-help; thrillers)
- 5.5" x 8.5" (general non-fiction; Sci-Fi; Business books)
- 6" x 9" (general fiction)
- 7" x 10" (reference books)
- 8.5" x 8.5" and 8" x 10" (children's books)
- 8.5" x 11" (textbooks)

If you want to do a photography book, the door is wide open for the format. Those types of books are produced as hardcover, often with an oblong format like 10" x 8" (bound on the 8" side) or even as large 12" x 12" square coffee table books.

INTERIOR MARGINS

The margins of a book are important. It takes into consideration the blank spaces around the printed content. Margins are also referred to as 'white space.'

The binding equipment can cut off content if the art or text is too close to the outer edge that will be trimmed. I've seen this before where text has been cut on the outer edges. That's because of poor design, ignoring template requirements.

For books with content that is mostly text, like a fiction novel, make sure there's enough white space in the gutter. The gutter is the center of a glued perfect bound book when open. If there's not enough white space, it will be hard for the reader to see and read the text toward the center of each page.

- The reader will tend to push the book in toward the spine to make it flatter. That can damage the glued binding over time.
- It can also be annoying, and I would not finish reading that book if it requires me to push the center to make the pages flatter because the text is too close to the gutter.

BLEEDS

Bleeds on a text page (interior) is a printing term used to describe the document with images or elements (a solid color) that touch the edge of the page, extending beyond the trim edge and *not* having a white margin. Having a white border can detract from the overall intended look.

When you design a page with a bleed, you don't have much space to work with. You will have three separate lines on the print document (it's a guide for the printer). You have the "safe zone," "cut lines," and "bleed area." Having a bleed requires the printer to use a larger sheet of paper and then trim it down after printing.

Accounting for bleed is an important part of graphic design because it helps create a clean edge on the finished product. A page bleed is not meant to be seen by the reader, only the printing plant.

You need to allow for ⅛" bleed; otherwise, any misalignment during the trim stage could result in the art not reaching the edge of the page.

Allowing for proper bleeds ensures that you get the results needed and the quality expected.

WHAT PAPER SHOULD I USE?

There are so many paper options, including coated or uncoated. Uncoated paper options include different types of finishes.

Book printers have standard paper options you can choose from. It's best to consider their options first since that will help keep costs down for your book project. That is important since the paper market is experiencing consolidation, affecting availability and lead time.

Examples are:

- Basis weights
  - o It's the weight of a sheet of paper based on standard size. In the US, we categorize paper types that way.

- o There's a range of options available for covers and text pages. Choose the right one for your book project
- o Here's a link for a basis paperweight chart - https://www.neenahpaper.com/resources/paper-101/basis-weights
- Uncoated paper
  - o Smooth finish
  - o Opaque finish - not as see-through and best for black and white photos
    - ▪ The opacity is higher (which reduces the passage of light)
  - o Vellum finish - gives the paper some bulk and has a rougher texture
  - o White or natural/cream
- Coated paper
  - o Best for color design and heavy ink coverage like covers
  - o Gloss finish - nice and shiny
  - o Matte finish - matte is easier on the eyes with heavy ink coverage
- Recycled paper
  - o Can be uncoated or coated
  - o Using recycled paper sends an important message about you (and your brand) being more sustainable.

Choosing paper is definitely connected to book formatting and affects the design of the book. Here are some questions to review with the designer:

- Is the interior text design just black and white?
- Are there photos? If so, are they black-and-white or 4-color?
  - o 4-color interior will increase the print cost, and you need to consider that for the retail price of your book.
- Does the design include 4-color or 2-color graphics on the interior text pages?
- Do the text pages have bleeds?

PREPARING YOUR BOOK FOR THE PRINTER

Excellent books are created when you send in great print-ready files for production. The designer is responsible for all this, but it doesn't hurt to know what they need to do when creating the graphic files for your book.

The book cover and interior pages need to be separate files when provided to the printer. Below is a list of what the standard requirements are for print-ready files.

COVER FILE PREP

1. Every book's spine width is different. The spine width is calculated using a formula that considers the number of pages in the book, the text paper stock thickness, and the binding style you selected in the book quote.

   a. If any of these factors change, please make sure to update the cover template you use.

2. Carefully proofread the manuscript once more before sending it to the printer.

   a. Corrections after the proofing stage costs money. $$$

3. Convert all colors to CMYK if printing with a 4-color process

   a. C = cyan
   b. M - magenta
   c. Y = yellow
   d. K = black

4. All fonts must be embedded in the print files.
5. Images must be 300 dpi.
6. Save black-and-white images in grayscale mode.
7. ⅛" minimum overlap for bleeds is required.
8. Your ISBN and barcode are on the back cover.

INTERIOR FILE PREP

1. Interior text PDF files must be in a single-page format and not in a two-page spread.
2. The number of pages in the book should end on an even number.
3. Left-side pages should be even-numbered, and right-side pages should be odd-numbered.
4. Blank pages should be included in the number of pages on your print quote.
5. A page equals each side of the paper. Each page of your PDF file counts as one page of your book. If your book has 200 pages, it will have 100 sheets of paper.
6. Page margins are the blank space around the edges of the page. In general, you insert text and graphics into a printable area between the margins.
7. All colors must be converted to CMYK.
8. All fonts must be embedded.
9. Images must be 300 dpi.
10. Save black-and-white images in grayscale mode.
11. ⅛" minimum for bleeds is required.
12. Your ISBN is listed on the copyright page.

PROOFING STAGE – ONE MORE CHANCE TO REVIEW THE CONTENT BEFORE PRINTING

The proofing stage is where the prepress department at the printing plant reviews the print files the designer provides. This is a very important step before your book goes to press.

The prep department will check and review the list mentioned above to make sure the print files are provided correctly. That process can take about forty-eight hours before getting the proof.

You can choose to view PDF proofs (which are digital) or physical proofs. I recommend you review both types of proofs for the first printing of a book.

A physical proof is the best way to see the book before it prints. That will ensure the books will print as intended by the design, any bleeds and trim look good, the pages are uniform, and no major errors were missed when reviewing the digital proof.

Make sure to include this extra time needed for a physical proof on your schedule because it will help establish the expected quality.

CHAPTER FIVE

MARKETING

IT'S ABOUT CREATING VALUE FOR YOUR BOOK

"Marketing starts with the first blank page."

~Honoree Corder

When people asked what my business major was while I was in college, I felt a little embarrassed sometimes to answer "marketing." Why did I feel that way? There was a connotation that marketers were sleazy. There were (and still are) some deceptive marketing approaches to get others to buy something that doesn't provide value to the buyer.

I view the purpose of marketing to build strong relationships; it also helps set the customer experience expectations. I've always been a people person and focusing on trust has helped with business development over my career.

The formal definition of marketing is the strategy involved in identifying and appealing to a particular group of consumers or partners. It's the activity and process for creating, communicating, and delivering offerings (products or services) that have *value*. It's about gaining attention too.

Marketing is an important aspect of publishing and can be hard because it's a never ending process. Think of marketing as your friend. Print media is a critical part of marketing strategies, and books fall into the print media category.

I have a marketing background but not a lot of marketing experience as a book author. There are a lot of subtleties in book publishing and the marketing that goes along with it.

HERE IS A SUMMARY OF WHAT BOOK MARKETING IS TO ME:

- Telling the right story upfront helps with the lifespan of your book.
- Make it evergreen content.
- Keep it in line with your brand and be consistent.
- Have an author platform. Make sure you have an SSL certificate for your website URL. This security step also conveys that your site can be trusted.
- Marketing changes all the time, so be flexible and adapt where needed.

- Consider the power of personalized print. You can license your content with others and create income from that.

Most authors are aware that you need a marketing plan for a book. But you need to understand it's not just about a marketing strategy. The plan must include tactics.   Marketing falls on the author's shoulders whether you are traditionally published or not.

I asked my friend, Lindsey Hartz, a few questions about book marketing. I've included excerpts of our conversation below. She specializes in helping authors market their books, whether they are independently published, hybrid published, or traditionally published. You can engage with Lindsey at https://www.hartzagency.com/

Brigitte: What are some simple marketing tactics an author should consider?

Lindsey: *Start with what makes you, you! Most authors I work with come to me with a list of what they can't do, what obstacles they are facing, and how overwhelmed they feel about the book marketing and launch process.*

We always work first on figuring out what natural talents, gifts, and communication style the author already has. Then we work to find marketing strategies that will allow the author to convey their message passionately in a way that feels comfortable to them. At the Hartz Agency, we have strengths in communication, persuasion, storytelling, and teaching that can be highlighted and used in any marketing campaign.

Next, make sure you are clear on who you are serving with your message, exactly how you are helping that audience, and what pain points or struggles that audience has around your book's message. This knowledge will help you craft marketing content that speaks directly to your future reader and compel them to buy because they are so invested in the transformation your work can bring to their life, business, faith, or situation.

Finally, don't try to do a marketing campaign alone. Reach out to friends, peers, and influencers who have the exact audience you are trying to reach. Make a generous offer to serve their audience with a brief teaching, an interview, or a free resource. Be sure to give that audience the next right step they can take with your book—for example, downloading a sample when they subscribe to your mailing list.

That will help you build an email list of interested people who will already have gotten to know you. Also, this small first interaction makes them more likely to buy the book when it becomes. available. In some cases, these people may become passionate advocates, spreading the word about your book to their friends, family, and network of associates.

Important note: When a friend, peer, or influencer helps you out in this way, make sure you do the same for them in the future.

Brigitte: **What benchmarks should an author consider for the reader's customer experience?**

Lindsey: *The main benchmark is always transformation. Can you help your reader get from point A to point Z with your work and help them experience change, growth, healing, or positive movement forward in their life, business, or situation?*

The whole point of a book is to tell a story that clearly outlines a situation you experienced, how you felt, the action you took, and the results you experienced. If you can bring your reader into your journey to not feel alone in their journey, and give them tangible hope mentally, physically, practically, or spiritually then you've succeeded!

The #1 takeaway about book marketing: It is ALWAYS the responsibility of the author to market and promote their book.

No publisher will market your book the way you want. No one cares as much as you.

PUBLISHING OPTIONS –

You may have noticed; I haven't mentioned the publishing options previously. How you publish a book is your choice as a writer. But no matter which publishing route is taken, the author needs to participate in the marketing process from start to end because it is intertwined.

This year, I decided to learn a bit more about the subtleties of book publishing by taking Honorée Corder's publishing course, *Publishing PhD*. Honorée is the author of fifty-three books. She has been highly successful and has learned a lot in her journey.

That course taught me how to market from an author's perspective, and it starts at the very beginning of the book idea. The different routes for publishing are: (1) independent (aka self publishing), (2) hybrid publishing, and (3) traditional publishing.

With independent and hybrid publishing, you keep the ownership of your intellectual property (IP). With traditional publishing, you assign your IP to the publisher. (Make sure to check before you sign to make sure you know who owns your content.)

Honorée's market focus is on indie publishers. Her guidance has been invaluable to me and many others, so I definitely recommend that you get guidance if you choose the indie route. That guidance will help you figure out how to make it happen. The upside is even though you take all the risk, you also make all the money.

With indie or self-publishing, you handle all the elements of the publishing process. Honoree is an expert at helping you learn that process so you don't end up making costly mistakes. https://honoreecorder.com

A hybrid publisher blends self-publishing with traditional publishing. They handle the production and help with marketing and distribution. There are a lot of hybrid publishers out there now that offer various packages, so be aware and compare models.

I met Karen Anderson through the course, and she works for a respected hybrid publisher, Morgan James Publishing where the author commits to purchasing books for their own use and the publisher pays a royalty fee for any books sold in the "trade." (The trade is defined as any retail market, online or off, like Amazon or Barnes and Noble stores, etc.).

Traditional publishing requires an agent accepting you as a client, and they pitch your idea to publishers to get you in the door. Traditional publishing has a high bar to be accepted and is slow and can be cumbersome to navigate.

In the 'old days' a traditional publisher paid high advances to an author. If you have a HUGE platform, they can still pay a high advance, but it can be challenging for first time authors. The way an advance works is really an "advance against royalties."

Many people feel like traditional publishing is the "Holy Grail." But the publishing world definitely changed when Amazon entered the picture.

In retrospect, when Amazon first came on the scene, the distributors and major publishing companies ignored Amazon and blew them off as a fad. The publishers were pretty ticked off as Amazon's influence grew and found the competition a little bit scary... because this gave authors more opportunities to get their message out there.

DISTRIBUTION METHODS – HOW TO GET YOUR BOOK OUT INTO THE MARKET

You made it this far!

Marketing is also connected to the distribution method you choose to take.

A lot of my clients have their own distribution channels based on their business niche. For companies, books are usually sold in bulk directly to other organizations or partners. For online marketers, they sell through social media or their own email list.

We still have a fulfillment perspective to deal with, and it varies with each project. This is an area where we partner with fulfillment companies to handle the inventory, packaging and shipping.

The definition of fulfillment in the publishing arena is the process of receiving an order, packing and shipping book orders. (Being an online bookstore and providing fulfillment is how Amazon got their foot in the publishing door.)

There are a lot of POD companies you can use that are also distribution platforms. The dominant ones are Kindle Direct Publishing (KDP) and IngramSpark. They compete against each other.

Distributing through KDP makes it easier to sell on Amazon because they are Amazon owned now. The trim sizes and paper offered for physical books are limited, but the process is easy if you want to self-publish and distribute there.

IngramSpark is a publishing site for indie authors using Lightning Source. Lightning Source is a sister company that targets experienced publishers with multiple titles. Your titles are available to be distributed to traditional bookstores through the Ingram Group. However, that does not necessarily mean a bookstore will carry your book using IngramSpark.

There are a lot of book distributors that can help get you into traditional bookstores and retail stores. These can have a high entry barrier. Independent Publishers Group is the original independent book distribution and sales company based in Chicago. https://www.ipgbook.com/

REUSE YOUR CONTENT FOR OTHER PRODUCTS

The content for your book is complete. So why not consider using it for other products?

eBooks

The design and layout of an eBook are important too. It requires an expert and involves much more than simply uploading a PDF file to KDP or other platforms. The layout is not the same as the printed version. Your designer definitely has some references if they can't assist with this.

Audiobooks

You have the book content. You might as well create an audio version. That requires proper recording equipment and editing software to have a high-quality audiobook. You, the author, can record yourself reading, or you can hire someone else to do the narration. It's up to you.

Amazon's audiobook division, ACX, is a great site to consider. https://www.acx.com/

Book into Film

"The book was better." That is a great slogan! It is one of my favorites and I had a t-shirt made with that slogan on the front. Filmmakers are also looking for great book content to turn into video content.

StoryRocket is an organization to promote your book to producers. https://www.storyrocket.com/

Online Courses

An online course is how many non-fiction authors, with an expertise focus, are re-using their content. For example, it's common (and easy) to take a chapter from a book and turn that into a lesson.

There are a lot of course platforms available and the one you use depends on the topic and teaching method. I recommend sending out a simple survey to your audience; that will clarify if they are interested in diving deeper into the content you write about and how they prefer to learn something.

- Do the learners want to watch videos for self-paced learning?
- Do the learners want to have interaction with the instructor on a regular basis?
- Do the learners want a group-based (cohort) learning experience?

Chapter Six

Reaching the Finish Line

We can all agree that writing, producing, and then marketing a book is hard. Let's not focus on how hard something is though. Instead, figure out how you can make it happen. You are an innovator.

I pointed out how digital print is expanding. Digital disruption has affected and changed every industry, including publishing, printing, and marketing. It's influence will continue to broaden.

I resisted embracing some of the print digital tech changes in the past too.

Digital innovation is the new rallying cry for everyone. We can learn a lot from tech companies because we need to be open to new ways of sharing content and distribution.

What is the one key characteristic of innovators? They are risk-takers. The tech startups are risk-takers, and so are the publishers. You are forced out of your comfort zone in many ways.

Publishers understand risk and have high entrepreneurial abilities too. Instead of blaming technology disruption for our problems, adapting to tech is needed to survive and thrive. We are all entrepreneurs and can use a variety of marketing methods to get our content seen.

The biggest takeaway I've learned with my print media experiences is this: ***collaboration and having a creative mindset helps develop ideas and solutions.*** That has become my manifesto.

Businesses, publishers, and authors come to me for advice on the best way to manufacture and produce their books for maximum ROI and high quality to align with their brand.

ROI is not just about *Return On Investment* but also provides a perspective of a *Return On Ideas*. I bring this up because sharing ideas in the process is important too. Without considering other ideas, progress isn't made. Make yourself open to options available for your situation.

You got this.

The Background of Print Media

I enjoy learning about history... so of course I have to share a little history about print and book production!

The printing press changed the world as much in the 15th Century as the internet is doing today.

Books gave everyone an opportunity to learn through reading. Books most likely generated strong emotions on both sides of an issue because they provided literacy to the whole world.

Books are the oldest form of print media. Access to books became easier when Gutenberg invented the mechanical process for printing them around 1440 in Germany.

Capital (access to money) is the one resource that printers did not have since they were considered craftsmen and moved around a lot to simply survive. It was very hard to secure a loan to open a print shop back then.

Books sold slowly because there were not many customers that could afford them. The only printers that succeeded for the long-term in setting up a business managed to find a financial backer.

I was a recent college graduate when the VP of Sales of a global book printer said this to me:

Brigitte, we can't consider you for the sales position in New York because, well, you're too nice, plus, you're a woman. We need you to help run and manage the Atlanta office.

That feedback motivated me to have more of an impact with books somehow.

Fast forward ten years when my role was Product Manager at Heidelberg Druckmaschinen in North America and the first female product manager at the global company. I'm very thankful to have played an integral part in the print media industry change in the 2000's.

A little background on Heidelberg. They developed the high-speed printing machine in 1856 and were the first company to market the idea globally. Heidelberg is headquartered in Heidelberg, Germany, and is globally known for high-quality equipment and solutions.

They have been successful in the long run because of the great design. They are innovative. Their products are useful; the presses look good and are efficient; and they are made to last a long time.

Their equipment is considered a good investment for quality print results. And underlying that good design is a culture that focuses on the customer's needs.

During World War I, Heidelberg's first live demonstrations had the 'Express' print machine mounted onto a car. It was driven to different printing companies in Germany to demonstrate how it worked. They sweetened the deal by allowing printers to buy their equipment and to pay by installments (essentially, a loan).

Where would the world be without those fast-printing presses? Heidelberg's business helped spread the idea of journalism, education, and printed communication by making the equipment affordable for the printers globally.

Heidelberg published a book in 2001 called *Handbook of Print Media: Technologies and Production Methods.* I have the English version on my bookshelf. It is over 1,200 pages, and my copy includes a CD attached to the inside back cover (the digital version of its time).

The *Handbook of Print Media* was released in the timeframe when I worked there, and the target audience was the graphic arts, printing, and publishing industries. It dove into offset printing, screen printing, digital prepress, electronic books, and production concepts.

So much has changed since 1856 (and 2001). Heidelberg has been adjusting to the ever changing market conditions. They have gradually integrated themselves into the overall process of print media. That's where I came in as one of three product managers for the North America market. We were responsible for the post-press equipment—cutters, folders, and stitching equipment.

Our basic message was: It doesn't matter how good the printing looks; if it is cut wrong or folded crooked, the end product will not look good. I worked closely with a liaison in Germany to create and update our message as needed for the North American market.

My first step was learning how the folding equipment worked at the Heidelberg factory headquarters in Germany. Reflecting on that makes me giggle. The folding supervisor didn't want me to touch the equipment; he thought I would hurt myself. I asked, "How the heck am I going to learn if I don't touch it?" (I'm a tactile learner.)

If you haven't picked up on it yet, the printing industry is male dominated. But the VP in the US (my boss at Heidelberg) thought I was smart and tough enough to handle it. I'm glad he gave me the opportunity and was grateful for his trust. Thank you, Larry Tanowitz, for believing this girl could handle it.

I digress. The launch of Heidelberg's new Post-Press Equipment Division was successful. As a global company, they understood that their approach needed to be adjusted for each geographic market (North America, South America, Asia, Europe, and Africa).

In North America, there were three of us working as a team to make sure the post-press message was consistent. Rob handled the cutters; Steve handled the stitching equipment; and I handled the folding equipment. We worked closely with the sales team, sales management, and were points of contact for the media.

Printing presses are very expensive. We're talking $10 million-plus for offset presses. The folding equipment was more in the $50,000 range. Heidelberg was the driving force behind all the expensive trade shows globally.

They spent a lot of money at trade shows. A lot. They even hired models. I was always picked to do the post-press presentations. A makeup artist was even hired for the models and me—they did our hair and make-up each morning. These trade shows were glitzy and glamorous.

Since 2005, the print industry has been in consolidation mode. Many plants have gone out of business when they couldn't find a partner or a buyout. The equipment investment is very expensive, even now.

The rise of digital technology has hurt companies like Heidelberg. Their market opportunity is shrinking fast.

Heidelberg's first adjustment was to buy Eastman Kodak's Office Imaging business, which got its foot in the digital print space. Back then, the industry thought Heidelberg was crazy getting into digital print. And Heidelberg had the used equipment market to contend with.

Heidelberg is now much different. The company has some deep roots in the print industry but had to adapt to the market requirements like everyone else. What keeps Heidelberg moving forward is the customer focus that top management emphasizes.

Heidelberg now offers workflow software solutions, prepress software, digital and offset equipment, post-press equipment, and added sustainability programs. Heidelberg has even narrowed their global print niche to commercial printers, packaging printers, and label printers. Is that going to be enough?

At least they recognize it's not just about equipment anymore. Heidelberg is still an integral part of a professional print media solution, but they no longer display at industry trade shows.

By the way, I did see the VP of Sales (the one who said I was too nice, and that wouldn't lead to success) at a book trade show in Manhattan ten years later. We conversed at the bottom of an escalator. He said, "Hi," and asked why I was there.

I wanted to show him the middle finger, but instead, smiled and nicely explained that I was one of the expert guest speakers at the book industry event.

MY BACKSTORY

I joke that I got into the book business by accident because money was needed to pay bills (rent and food) and for college tuition on my own. At the time, it also seemed that I was drifting—trying to find a purpose in life and for even attending college. That's another story.

I eventually applied for a job opportunity in the local newspaper after moving to Wisconsin. The role that resulted ended up being one that provided focus and became my favorite job as a college student.

It was working for a respected and very large book printer, Banta, whose clients included many prominent New York publishers. (Banta was eventually acquired by RR Donnelley, the largest global book printing organization.)

Side note: When I got the phone call from HR to schedule an interview, I wasn't aware there was a difference between book printing and publishing. I thought they were the same thing because, back then, many traditional publishers printed their books at their own printing plants.

That call for an interview with the book printer changed my life; it was a catapult into the book industry. My first responsibilities at Banta were simply answering the phones and typing transcripts. I was one hell of a fast typist and accurate.

Then they trusted me to start delivering faxes to executives. Faxes were a big deal then and were considered high priority, secure, and urgent. Fax machines were a new type of communication technology, faster than the post office, before email and texting with mobile phones replaced it.

The fax machine was in the company mailroom, and when a fax came in, someone from the mailroom came to let me know. I usually had to pause what I was doing in order to deliver it. If the cover letter stated "confidential" that made me more curious; I would quickly scan the fax content. Don't tell anybody.

I started to learn about every aspect of the book production process by chatting with the executives and asking questions of the pressroom management. They appreciated the curiosity from a college student, a girl with a southern accent living in Wisconsin.

Thankfully, the company invested in their employees and helped pay for my college classes based on a minimum GPA each semester. For a new inexperienced employee like me, that was a definite motivator to learn more and study hard.

Banta eventually moved me into assistant roles in different departments. Prepress, customer service, marketing, sales, and accounting. Yes, accounting. My business major was in marketing and economics.

Those roles were a way to assess my skills and eventually led to new assignments such as flying to in-person meetings with a high-level sales rep to meet clients in person. I enjoyed customer-facing roles the best. My fondness for books was on display at each meeting.

This process I went through is now called a paid internship. It's a great way for a company to test the potential of a staff member in a complex system like the business of books.

Print industry consolidation started to become a thing and Banta was buying other book printing plants in the early 1990s. Once I graduated from college, they offered me an opportunity to help manage a new office in Denver or Atlanta. I was open to either location. They decided to only open a new office in Atlanta. That location was basically a consolidation of the sales reps from the different print plants.

I later went to work for a traditional publisher, Western Publishing, which also had its own book printing plants globally. Their most popular titles were in the *Little Golden Books* series. My role was to manage current accounts and find client opportunities to use the press equipment because of available press time.

Did you know that IBM published children's books at one point? I did a lot of press checks with them.

That was also around the time when email became popular and provided more flexibility for work. It was a major tool to help communicate faster with clients and fellow employees. My life at home was changing as well. As a new mom, having access to email allowed me to start working remotely and not have to deal with daily commutes to the office in between traveling. Hallelujah!

I worked for a couple of other book printers and then with Heidelberg in a marketing role (product management) for North America. Then I was recruited by a startup, InnerWorkings, that disrupted the print industry even more. We focused on corporate clients and offered multiple communication solutions. That independent contractor role lasted over a decade.

More recently I was at Pitney Bowes in a business development position that focused on digital platforms for communications. Guess what? That division was sold to a private equity firm and many jobs were eliminated, including mine.

I felt I was just a little bit ahead of a tsunami with all the consolidations continuing to happen.

Three months after the layoff in 2014, I had to deal with a second cancer diagnosis. Unbelievable, right? I was honest with sharing what was happening to my inner circle. One of my clients advocated and convinced me to start my own business because of the mutual trust we had developed.

That cancer reality was unexpected and continuing to help others provided much-needed confidence and some freedom. So I started my own company, Gemini Media, as a full-time pursuit.

Over the years, I have learned that building a stronger muscle for empathy, communication, and asking for help has contributed to trust and credibility. This allows me to share knowledge, help develop solutions, and make an impact.

Brigitte Cutshall ~The Book Girl

Let's Wrap It Up

"A brand is what other people say about you when you're not in the room."

~Jeff Bezos

As an author, branding is both how your book is viewed by the public and yourself as the writer. It's also what people think and believe about you.

I truly hope that reading this book has inspired and motivated you to finish that book you've been thinking about. And to make it a professionally published excellent book.

Based on feedback while writing this, I created a Quality Book Formula checklist to help motivate others by simplifying the process. (The goal in creating the checklist was to provide guidance on the expected overall timeline.)

You can download "Quality Book Formula Checklist" PDF for free at

https://qualitybookformula.com

I'm in the process of creating some videos related to the *Quality Book Formula* content and will dive a little deeper into questions that are sent to me. The video links will be posted on the Quality Book Formula site. My goal is to provide more guidance on how to professionally publish your book for excellence!

RECOMMENDED BOOKS TO MOTIVATE YOU

Bird by Bird, by Anne Lamott

You Must Write a Book, by Honoree Corder

Project Management for Writers, by Terry Stafford

The Copyright Handbook, by Stephen Fishman

This is Marketing, by Seth Godin

Market Like a Boss, by Honoree Corder

You Are the Brand, Mike Kim

ABOUT THE AUTHOR

Brigitte Cutshall is a media solutions and production expert, focused on delivering the best solutions to content creators. She is the founder of Gemini Media, the host of *Real Things Living Podcast*, and a health advocate. Brigitte is an accomplished business development professional in the communications, publishing, and print management industry.

Thank you for purchasing the

QUALITY BOOK FORMULA!

There are more books to come…

OTHER BOOKS BY BRIGITTE:

- *Real Things: 6 Ways to Embrace Life* (2015)
- *Expecting the Good: Inspiration from a Badass with a Big Heart* (2018)
- *At the Helm* (co-author, Fiction) (2019)
- *Real Things Living Coloring Journal: Add Some Color to Your Life* (2020)

HOW TO STAY IN TOUCH:

- Sign up for the newsletter at brigittecutshall.com
- Connect on Instagram @brigittecutshall
- Connect on LinkedIn: linkedin.com/brigittecutshall
- Subscribe to the YouTube Channel: youtube.com/realthingsliving
- Subscribe and Listen to *Real Things Living Podcast*: brigittecutshall.com/podcast

  - Distributed on iHeartRadio, Apple Podcasts, Audible, and Spotify

Acknowledgements

This book would not have happened without the input from other people.

There are so many people to thank. Most important is the support from my family: my husband, Carl; my sons, Hudson and Jacob; my sister, Michele; my brother, John; and my mom, Alexandrine.

The idea to create and write about this particular topic came from connecting with other authors and actually listening to their advice. *I took my own knowledge for granted*. Thank you to Karen Anderson, Honoree Corder, Terry Stafford, Fredrick Haugen, Lindsey Hartz, and Dino Marino. Every single one of them provided valuable feedback and motivation.

And a BIG Thank You to the clients who continue to support my business endeavors and to make sure I'm not bored.

&NDORSEMENTS

Brigitte is an expert in a field that was once common, but no more...prepress and production of books. Not only does she know what she's talking about, but in our 20 years of working together, she's made more clients happy than I can count. If you want your book production process to improve, be more efficient and probably save you money, this is your read.

~ **Chris Rank**, *Rank Studios*

I have been working with Brigitte for four years personally. She has been a wealth of resource to our company. A repository of knowledge – she has never steered us wrong. She has always offered detailed expertise and solutions on how to produce our books cost-effectively and efficiently. So you've written the book – that is only half the battle. The printing process is detailed, with many moving parts, and Brigitte provides the necessary insight into the "how to's" of printing.

~ **Erika Andujar**, *OneHope International*

Whatever problem has been presented, we have been able to count on Brigitte for over two decades to find the most cost effective and productive solutions. Premium Press America has been recognized by a variety of industry associations with the highest honors…honors that we share with Brigitte. The variety of publications relative to the needs of our customers in terms of quantity, size, format, cover material, paper, retail price was made possible by the expertise and genuine interest of Brigitte.

~*George Schnitzer Jr.*, *Publisher at Premium Press America*

Brigitte is a master of creating and holding space for others to explore the edges of their understanding and ability to step into their potential. The depth of her knowledge and her drive to help others is what makes her work compelling and impactful.

~*Scott Perry*, *Chief Difference-Maker at Creative on Purpose*

Working with Brigitte was a very pleasant experience. She is a thorough professional who works with deceptive ease. She gets things moving smoothly because of her focus and understanding of the objective. She is also a wonderful person to know apart from her professional prowess.

~ *Anurag Gupta*, *Director of Total Application Software*

Brigitte has shown herself to be a phenomenal manager of projects that I have worked with her on. She takes on every project as if it is her own, and the evidence of that is in the details.

*~**Anthony Sylvester,** Jr., Vice President at Interface Consulting*

I couldn't get enough of Quality Book Formula! As someone who for all practical purposes preaches about publishing a quality book, I was cheering Brigitte on throughout the pages of her book, all while learning new things myself. Having a book that is a perennial seller requires it to be well-thought out, professionally published, and yes, top quality. Get Quality Book Formula so you'll know all of the boxes to check to ensure your book is a long-term winner!

*~**Honorée Corder,** Strategic Book Coach & Author of 53 best-selling books including You Must Write a Book*

GLOSSARY

Audiobooks

- Amazon's audiobook division - ACX - https://www.acx.com
- Audiobook distribution to support local bookstores - https://libro.fm/

Books into Film

- https://www.storyrocket.com

Book Marketing Agency

- https://www.hartzagency.com

Brand protection on Amazon

- https://brandservices.amazon.com

Distribution options for Independent Publishing

- KDP - https://kdp.amazon.com
- IngramSpark - https://www.ingramspark.com/
- Independent Publishers Group - https://www.ipgbook.com

Paper weight options

- https://www.neenahpaper.com/resources/paper-101/basis-weights

Registrations

- Copyright - https://copyright.gov
  - o Download details of copyright basics in the U.S. https://www.copyright.gov/circs/circ01.pdf
- ISBN - https://isbn.org
- Library of Congress - https://loc.gov/publish

Strategic Book Coach

- https://honoreecorder.com/

REFLECTIVE NOTES

- Include EFH's Pricing Estimates
- Give the people want they want, prices
  and recommendations
- High-level details on press ready files
- Print companies
- Design. What are large spaces
  between words?
- What's up with these MASSIVE
  lined pages? Book Experts?
- Shitty Copyeditor
- No consistent headers, and
  proofreader at a 4 year old lvl

Made in United States
Troutdale, OR
10/03/2023

13382892R00065